GW00724918

Tippers

A play

Gillian Plowman

Samuel French – London
New York – Sydney – Toronto – Hollywood

HN38990

TIPPERS

First performed by the Flat Four Players, with the following cast:

Annette	Lorna Fletcher
Durrell	Simon Allen
Col	Derek Benfield
Arthur King	David Flint
Teresa	Karrie Stark

The play was produced by Gillian Plowman

The action of the play takes place on a tip in Birmingham over one day

CHARACTERS

Annette, blonde, pregnant, 28
Durrell, Irish, unemployed, 32
Col, offender, mad on football, 24
Arthur King, divorced, unemployed, 40
Teresa, divorced, defiant, mother of five, 33.

The play could take place in any appropriate city, if the football references are altered accordingly. If wished, the names of the footballers may be up-dated.

TIPPERS

A tip in Birmingham. Morning

Seagulls call as a mist rises off the tip. The Lights come up to silhouette all five characters as they search and fill sacks and bags. Annette, Durrell and Teresa recede and remain in silhouette whilst Col and Arthur are lit DS

Col It's a really good boot this. Buggered if I can find the other one.

Arthur Give us. (*He empties some gunge out of the boot*) Size ten. Do me.

Col Do me an' all.

Arthur Find us the other one.

Col I'm bloody lookin'.

Col holds out his hand for the boot but Arthur puts it in his own bag

You want it, you can find the other one yourself.

Arthur clouts Col

Arthur Do as you're told, right.

Col sees the other boot and hands it over silently

Villa at home this week?

Col Yeah.

Arthur Sell that lot and you can go.

Col I'll get it to the van. Thanks, Arthur.

Col picks up three plastic sacks and a pushchair and staggers off with them. He can't manage the pushchair and drops it

Teresa comes downstage. She picks up the pushchair and defies Col. Col looks menacing. Teresa stands her ground

Col Arthur!

Arthur approaches

Teresa Hello, Arthur.

Arthur No women allowed on the tip.

Teresa I know that. No men, neither.

Arthur No women.

Teresa Says who?

Col Arthur King. He says.

Arthur Give him his pushchair back.

Teresa Says Arthur King. Here you are, baby.

Col I'll get you.

Arthur Shut up, Col.

Col No women allowed.

Teresa turns her back and walks away. Col runs after her and pushes her over. He looks at Arthur for approval

No women.

Arthur Get it to the van and don't take all day. There's a couple more beasts on the horizon—we'll see what they've got.

Col staggers off

You want to get buried.

Teresa Little shit. What's he? Delinquent or something?

Arthur I keep Colin out of trouble.

Teresa Not entirely, I wouldn't say.

Arthur I haven't had him long.

Teresa Where did you get him from?

Arthur Answered an advert. Rehabilitation of offenders. They pay you board and lodging.

Teresa Maybe I'll get one. Maybe not.

Arthur gives Teresa a hand up

Arthur Get off the tip.

Teresa You not heard of equality, Arthur? I've got a living to make and all.

Arthur It's dangerous.

Teresa I'm brave.

Arthur I don't care if you get churned up, kid. We all got to die sometime. One way or another. But any horrible, nasty accidents like that, and we'll all be run off.

Teresa Trust me, Arthur.

Arthur does a foot and arm twist and grounds her. He keeps his foot on her

Arthur Dangerous, you see.

Teresa My grandmother used to make mats with rags. Cut them into little bits and knotted them through a hessian backing. She did some lovely one. Lots of colours. And she could remember where all the bits came from. "You've just spilt your orange juice on my best dress", she would say, and I would look at her, and she'd be pointing to one of her mats. They lasted for years. It's a thought, isn't it. Rag mats. Could become all the rage in the posh shops.

Arthur Rubbish tip rag mats?

Teresa They'd never know. Washed, they'd never know. Take a bloody long time though. Winter evening job. You just need an idea, you see, Arthur. I could make silk and satin rag mats for bedrooms. Start me own business. Fancy a partnership?

Arthur Done that.

Teresa Had your own business?

Arthur Fruit and veg. Shop and van. With my wife. My ex-wife.

Teresa We're all divorced, Arthur.

Arthur You talk about equality. She was up to her neck in lovers, whilst I was slaving till all hours selling off the back of me van. Then, when she'd decided she wanted to be an independent woman, I had to sell up, and give her the lot so that she and the kids could live a decent life. Whatever I earn—that's a laugh—goes in maintenance, and she does fuck all. That's her being independent.

Teresa Well at least you know you've done the best by your kids.

Arthur They could be anybody's.

Teresa Can I get up now?

He lets her up

Teresa I'll tell you something, King Arthur. If I'd been your wife, I'd have done exactly the same.

Arthur Get off my patch.

Teresa I don't see a sign.

Arthur No women.

Teresa If I come across a round table, I'll let you know.

Arthur If I come across any silk or satin, I'll let you know.

Teresa Why?

Arthur I'd like to see you dressed in silk and satin. What's your name?

Teresa Mother Teresa. (*She gives him a rude sign and moves* US)

Col comes in DS

Durrell, who has a bottle of Guinness, joins Col

Col
Durrell   (*singing together*) Here we go *etc*

Col Arthur, there's a load been dumped. Looks all right. It'll go on top of the van. Hardly needs drying out. We can get it straight down to Nobby's. You're not having none, Durrell.

Durrell It's all right for you. There's two of you. And you got a bleedin' van. You must be making a fortune.

Col Over a hundred quid yesterday ...

Arthur slaps Col

I was only telling him ...

Arthur He doesn't want to know.

Durrell Can't I come in with you. Use your van?

Arthur I'll tell you. Paddy. You start with a cart ...

Durrell I haven't got a cart.

Arthur You make a cart. Pram wheels will do. You pull it along, like you was a kid, Durrell. And you load it up. And you pull it to a purchaser. Now, you make enough money, you can hire the van. One full load for twenty pounds. But I want it back within the hour.

Durrell I got to load it.

Arthur Or you can save a bit more and put down a deposit on your own van.

Durrell Yeah. (*He opens another bottle of Guinness from his pocket*)

Arthur Or you can spend it all on booze. Lead! (*He picks up a piece of lead sheeting*)

Durrell Get a bit for that. (*He searches for more*)

Arthur Fuck off, Durrell.

Durrell Hey ...

Arthur Fuck off!

Arthur and Col go out

Durrell calls to one of the figures US

Durrell Nette!

Annette comes towards him. She is pregnant

What you got?

Annette Where've you been?

Durrell Getting here.

Annette Two hours getting here?

Durrell I had business.

Annette What business?

Durrell Discussing with a guy about buying a van.

Annette What for?

Durrell Get the stuff back.

Annette You ain't got any stuff.

Durrell You have. You should have. What've you got?

Annette Nothing.

Durrell Nothing?

Annette No, nothing.

Durrell You been here two hours.

Annette And I can't find anything.

Durrell There's a heaving great mass of stuff. What's the matter with you, you can't find anything?

Annette Everything's dirty.

Durrell Yeah, right. It's dirty. That don't matter. It's dirty for Christ's sake. You take it home and clean it down. You put it in the yard, Annette, and you hose it down.

Annette You do it. You don't do anything.

Durrell I'm negotiating for a van.

Annette Durrell, you're always negotiating, but you never settle anything. We never get anywhere. You never got a job. We never got married. We never moved out of your mother's crumbling house.

Durrell They don't know she's dead.

Annette 'Course they know she's dead. THEY buried her.

Durrell Don't, Annette. The shame of it will last me to me own grave. That I never had the money to bury her.

Annette You drink all your money, Durrell.

Durrell I do not! Don't you say that. I have the odd drink for me pleasure, because there's no pleasure else.

Annette Not with me?

Durrell There's no sex now is there? There's nothing but a rough-edged tongue. Irish women aren't like that. They're soft . . .

Annette In the head if they turn out men like you.

Durrell It's not my fault there's no work, is it?

Annette You don't know the meaning of the word.

Durrell You apologise for that remark, woman.

Annette You waste so much of your life gassing.

Durrell You apologise.

Annette There's a cooker over there. I'll help you get it. It was too heavy for me on me own. If you can get a price for it, I can go to the supermarket. I'm dying to go to the supermarket.

Durrell Say you're sorry.

Annette I'm sorry.

Durrell You didn't mean it.

Annette I did.

Durrell You just said it.

Annette You told me to.

Durrell Apologise for saying I don't work.

Annette You don't bloody work.

Durrell All my life I've wanted to work. There's nothing to do.

He hurts her. She shouts. Teresa turns

Annette I'm sorry, Durrell, it's this baby. It makes you a bit odd sometimes, having a baby. I hope it's a boy, Durrell. You can take him to the football . . .

Teresa When was Villa first admitted to the League?

Durrell Eighteen eighty-eight.

Teresa What year did they win the European cup?

Durrell Nineteen eighty-one to eighty-two.

Teresa He's good.

Annette Oh yes, he's good at his football. He could have been a footballer. You could, couldn't you, Durrell? It was his eyesight that let him down. He could have been rich and famous.

Teresa You couldn't help me, could you? I've got a barrow over there.

Annette He's very kind, Durrell is.

Durrell Sure, sure. Trouble with you women, you just haven't got the physical attributes for the job.

Teresa Strong arms, broad shoulders, stamina . . .

Durrell And no sense of smell!

He laughs and shoulders her goods. Teresa nods to Annette

Teresa All right?

Annette Yes, thanks.

Durrell Hey, you wouldn't lend us your barrow, would you? Get a few things down the road, like. I'm negotiating, you see. If I can pick up twenty quid this morning, I can hire this bloke's van for an hour this afternoon, and if I make enough, I'll take the wife out tonight.

Annette For a pizza, Durrell?

Durrell To the pub for a steak. You've got to eat for two now, you know.

Annette (*to herself*) So long as you don't drink for two.

Durrell and Teresa exit

Col enters and goes to the cooker

Annette looks up to see Col standing by her cooker

That's mine.

Col No label on it.

Annette I just came to get me husband.

Col I don't see him.

Annette He's gone to help somebody.

Col That's his pigeon.

Annette He'll kill me. I haven't got anything yet.

Col Women aren't allowed on the tip.

Annette I have to do what he says. He's my husband. You tell HIM.

Col I will.

Annette I will.

Col I said I will.

Annette Sounds like a wedding.

Col What?

Annette I will.

Col I wouldn't. Arthur says not to. Women bleed you dry, Arthur says.

Annette Women bleed for men.

Col Are you having a baby?

Annette Yes.

Col A little one?

Annette It's quite little. Durrell was negotiating for ages. I thought it would never happen. I think it's because he drinks a lot and it gets diluted.

Col What?

Annette What you need.

Col Right.

Annette You know him, don't you. Durrell?

Col Paddy. Yeah.

Annette I've seen you in the pub together.

Col Haven't seen you.

Annette I wait outside sometimes. Make sure he gets home. He's a liability, my husband. You married?

Col I told you.

Annette Do you live on your own?

Col With Arthur.

Annette I see.

Col It's not like that. I was advertised. Not like that!

Annette Well, I've never seen any Arthurs waiting outside for you . . .

Col His wife walked out on him and I walked in.

Annette Convenient.

Col He makes me do things.

She looks at him

Cooking. Ironing. Stuff.

Annette Walk out then.

Col I'd have to be advertised all over again. I'm taking that cooker. He'll be pleased with me.

Annette groans

What's the matter?

Annette It moves about. Gets in an awkward position.

Col Sit down then.

There is nowhere to sit. There is machine noise. The lights dim to indicate danger

Annette I've got to get the cooker before it gets covered.

Col We'd better move before we get covered.

Annette No! I've got to get it.

He pulls her away as the noise gets deafening. Black-out. The cooker is covered. The noise stops. Lights up

Annette It's gone.

Col What about the little baby?

Annette It was better than the one in my house. I've scrubbed and scrubbed it but it's done too many Irish stews and it won't come clean. And it won't cook right. It's damp, our house.

Col Ours is.

Annette It's not right for a baby though, is it?

Col Can't you get re-housed?

Annette He won't go and ask.

Col You go then.

Annette No. I found a box on the tip last week. Just stumbled on it. I had a sort of feeling about it. Little wooden thing with varnished paint on—not broken or anything. So I took it straight home and cleaned it. Do you know, there was a name on it—Agnes Maskell, eighteen ninety-six. As clear as clear. It was lovely—I wanted to keep it. But I can't keep anything, 'cos he'll take it and sell it. He's good at selling things. He just won't find anything. The antique man gave me ten pounds for it and I bought two little suits for the baby. I wrapped them carefully and I got them out every day to air, but this morning, they had mould on.

Arthur enters

Col turns to face Arthur

Arthur Women aren't allowed on this tip, Col.

Col I told her.

Arthur Women are a waste of time.

Col My mother was a woman. She was all right. She looked after me.

Arthur Then how come you spent so much time inside?

Col It wasn't her fault I nicked things. She'd have thrashed me if she'd known. I got in with a bad lot.

Arthur I bet she moaned when you wanted to go and watch football . . .

Col She didn't

Arthur A saint, was she?

Col She loved football. My first memory of me mother was her and me kicking a ball about our kitchen. Every time she was pregnant she used to tell me she had a football under her dress. Hey, Arthur! A football! A bleeding football. (*He looks up*) Thanks, Ma. "Here we go, here we go" (*etc*). Come on Arthur.

He kicks the ball about and Arthur joins in

Durrell enters, smoking a cigarette, and joins in. He coughs and splutters

Teresa enters. She has a harness around her neck with bags on it, which she is loading

Teresa (*to Annette*) Get off home.
Annette I've got to help him.
Arthur Wood.
Col Wood?
Arthur I've been doing it on me own so far.
Col I've done it so far.

Arthur clips Col's ear

You've done most of it, Arthur. I expect I could have done a bit more.
Durrell Do him good. (*He takes a drink from his hip flask*)

Col clouts Durrell

Col and Arthur move off

Annette comes DS *and Durrell hits her instead of Col*

Do you good and all. Nette. Oh, Nette, I'm sorry, darlin'. It was the little bugger I meant to hit.
Annette If you hit me again, I'll lose this baby.
Durrell Don't you threaten me. You'd better have that baby or else. That's my immortality, that is—him and his son, and his . . .
Annette If you want me to have this baby, then why aren't I at home, cosy, warm and well-fed, whilst you're out breadwinning?
Durrell I don't feel very well.
Annette It's hitting women, that is. It makes you feel bad.

Arthur and Col carry across a single wardrobe

Col Why do people throw away wardrobes, Arthur? That's the second one this month. Walnut, isn't it?

Arthur Bloody big walnut.

Col It's heavy.

Arthur You've only got half of it.

Col Half of it's heavy.

Arthur I've got the heavy half.

Arthur and Col exit

Durrell sinks to the ground

Annette You don't feel well because we live in a damp house and sleep in damp sheets. Why don't you go to the council?

Durrell I feel sick, Nette.

Annette You've gone green.

Durrell Green?

Annette And purple. You all right?

Durrell I can't get me breath.

Annette Blotchy. All different shades.

Durrell groans. Annette treads over to Teresa

Excuse me.

Teresa You're daft, you are.

Annette Me husband. He's gone coloured.

Teresa Has he. Why?

Annette He's sick, I think.

Durrell groans loudly. They return and inspect him

He's blue now.

Teresa He could be having a heart attack.

Annette He's Irish.

Teresa How important is he?

Annette Not very, really. It's his eyesight.

Teresa He's your husband.

Annette Nearly.

Teresa Good one?

Annette He's the only one I've nearly got.

Teresa I've never had a good one.

Annette How many you had?

Teresa Four.

Annette Four! I don't believe you.

Teresa I was going to be a granny soon, but my daughter had an abortion.

Annette And I'm not even a mother yet.

Teresa I was only thirteen when Sally was born. My parents were good. They let us live at home till I was sixteen. Then I started getting married. The first one got fat. You don't want a fat husband, darling, they're lazy. The second was unfaithful. Normal, you might think, but he was unfaithful on my family allowance. The third wanted excitement and got killed being a mercenary in Africa somewhere, so I suppose he got it. And the fourth was French.

Annette What's wrong with that?

Teresa Garlic mainly. And a limited vocabulary.

Annette I can't speak French.

Teresa You don't live in France.

Annette Durrell's none of those things.

Teresa You want to keep him then?

Annette Yes.

Arthur and Col return

Teresa King Arthur! Give us a hand.

Arthur What's the matter with him?

Durrell Pains. (*He clutches himself and collapses*)

Col Hey, Paddy, here we go, here we go, here we go . . .

Teresa We'll have to get him off the tip.

Arthur We'll have to get him off the tip.

Col Villa one, Portsmouth nil.

Arthur and Col take an arm each

Teresa Take his leg. What's your name?

Annette Annette.

Col She's having a little baby. She shouldn't be lifting heavy things. Legs are heavier than arms.

Teresa No they're not.

Col They're bigger.

Col and Annette swop

Teresa The legs are further from the body. If you've got the arms, you've got the body as well.

Col and Annette swop back again. Teresa and Arthur swop. They cannot lift Durrell and he cries out

Teresa We need a stretcher.
Arthur Something flat to carry him on.
Teresa A stretcher.
Arthur Not necessarily.
Annette Call an ambulance.
Teresa We will do when we get him off the tip.
Col (*singing*) "Good old Nigel, Nigel's the one." The wardrobe! We could put him in that.
Arthur That's flat. And it's not a stretcher, see.

Arthur and Col exit

Durrell Goal!

He slumps again. The noise of a machine starts and the lights dim a little

Annette Durrell!
Teresa Shit!

Arthur and Col rush on with the wardrobe. They put the wardrobe down on its side and roll Durrell into it, turning it on its back as the Lights dim further. They scrabble to move the wardrobe as a Black-out denotes the passing of a truck. The Lights come up. Annette is in a state

Arthur Let's see what's new, Col.

Arthur goes off

Teresa Lie down, Annette, and put your feet up. Higher than your head. Just in case. Don't want to take no chances.

Annette lies on the wardrobe and groans

That's right. Just relax a little.
Arthur (*off*) Col!
Teresa You warm enough?

Col takes his coat off and puts it over Annette

You're a nice boy.
Col I'm not! I'm not a nice boy at all!

Arthur (*off*) Col!

Col I have to be kept in order. (*He wanders around, but keeps coming back to continue the conversation*) I pushed you over, didn't I? That wasn't nice. My mother would have thrashed me. I'm a thug.

Annette I'm not going to lose it, am I? I've got terrible back pains.

Teresa You'll be all right.

Col When I was a kid, I stole things.

Teresa Yes?

Annette Have you got kids?

Teresa Yes.

Annette How many?

Teresa Five. One off each husband and Sally.

Col Off other kids.

Teresa All kids steal at some time or other.

Col Off me mum.

Teresa Part of growing up.

Annette I'm worried about one. Where do you get the money from to raise kids?

Teresa I'll tell you. Stick to one and it won't be so bad.

Col Off little kids. Littler than me.

Annette I couldn't do that. He'll need brothers and sisters round, or he'll end up getting done in by the other kids. It's no good being an only one.

Teresa Mine don't look after each other.

Col I tried to drown me brother once.

Teresa Always fighting, my boys.

Col I had to take him to school. He was littler than me.

Annette And there's no jobs. It's not right to bring kids into the world when there's no jobs for them.

Col I hated school. I didn't go. He told on me.

Teresa Sally's training to be a teacher.

Col I hate teachers!

Annette gets up and throws off the coat

Annette Perhaps I shouldn't have this one.

Teresa Sit down.

Col He's over six foot now ... (*He jumps into the air, punching an imaginary face*)

Teresa Who?

Col My brother.

Annette jumps up and down on top of the wardrobe

Annette See, little baby, there's nothing for you on the outside
except two mouldy baby-gros and me for a mother.
Teresa Annette, you're a wonderful person ...

Col is fighting with his imaginary brother

Col Everybody's bigger than me ...
Teresa Colin, you're a wonderful person ...

Arthur appears

Sort him! (*To Annette*) You'll be a wonderful mother.
Arthur That's it! You and me! Finished! You haven't done a
stroke all day, because you will insist on talking to women. I
told you, didn't I, they'd be the ruin of you, you stupid little
bugger.
Col I'm not little! (*He jumps on Arthur's back with a stranglehold*)

*The following dialogue overlaps as the Director wishes, so that there
is a cacophony of sound*

Arthur I've loaded the van, it's all mine. I'm going to sell it, and
you can move out of the house ...
Col I loaded the van. You're not getting a penny, Arthur Bloody
King of the Fairies, and you can move out of the house and I'm
going to fill it with women and I'm gonna screw them all ...
Annette There's no point in getting born, baby, 'cos it's all rubbish
on the outside ...

*She continues to jump up and down on the wardrobe, and Col
continues to pummel Arthur*

Teresa I loved every one of my babies, Annette. You go and have
as many as you like.

*Annette stops jumping, and Arthur and Col fall to the ground at the
same time. There is a lull in the chaos, and a banging from inside the
wardrobe*

Silence

Durrell Help!

They watch with fascination as the door of the wardrobe opens and Durrell climbs out

Jesus. Mary, Mother of God. I thought I was buried alive.

Annette Are you all right, Durrell?

Durrell No.

Col We saved you from the machine.

Durrell I'm black and blue all over.

Arthur (*to Col*) You nearly killed me.

Col Sorry, Arthur.

Arthur I'm going to re-advertise you.

Col (*to Teresa*) I'm not nice.

Teresa offers Arthur a hand up, much to his surprise

Teresa It's people that are trouble, Arthur. Not women. Not men. People.

Col I shall find something brilliant.

Col exits

Durrell I can't see anything.

Annette It's 'cos you've been in the dark.

Durrell I've had a bang on the head.

Annette I suppose babies can't see when they come out.

Durrell They don't get banged on the head.

Annette I've got to put me feet up, Durrell. The baby's at risk.

Durrell They get banged on the bottom.

Annette lies back on the wardrobe and puts her feet up

Where's me flask? Get off! I've lost me flask!

Annette No.

Durrell Get off! Oh …

He sits down heavily on the wardrobe

Annette Durrell?

Durrell Joseph and Mary, Nette. I feel rough.

Annette We'll go home.

Durrell I wanted to get some money, Nette, to take you out.

Annette We'll stay in.

Annette strokes Durrell's head. Teresa picks up her shoulder bags full of stuff

Arthur You're a strong 'un.
Teresa Yeah? Now I am independent, Arthur.

Arthur takes the bags off her

Me barrow's over there.

They move off

Durrell notices the wardrobe

Durrell Hey, this is all right. I could sell this. Get the other end.
Annette I can't.
Durrell Nette!
Annette I'm losing this baby.
Durrell I've lost me hip flask. I'm not making a fuss, am I?
Annette Yes, you are. And it's not important. The baby's important.
Durrell It doesn't look lost to me.

Durrell starts to drag the wardrobe, falls ill and collapses into it. Annette shuts the door on him and stands looking at it. She opens the door again

Annette If it's a girl we could call her after your mother. Would she have your surname or mine? Eileen Smith. Eileen Dolan. Eileen Smith. Eileen Dolan.

She begins to cry and sits on the wardrobe

Col comes in and offers her a drink from Durrell's hip flask

Col I nicked it.
Annette He nicked it.

Pause

He's gone coloured again. He can't look after me. I don't know what I'm going to do.
Col I found something.
Annette What?

Col holds out a piece of broken china

It's broken.
Col It's real china. If you hold it up to the light, you can see through it.

Annette It's just a bit.

Col There's a whole rose on it.

Annette Nobody'll buy it.

Col You're very beautiful.

Annette I'm not.

Col You are.

Annette I'm fat and ugly.

Col I'm thin and spotty.

Annette Yes.

Col I'd love to be tall, dark and handsome.

Annette Tall, willowy and rich.

Col Live in a palace ...

Annette With marble statues and a swimming pool.

Col And a football pitch.

Annette Marble statues and a football pitch.

Col Marble statues of Nigel Spink, Allan Evans, Tony Daley, Bernard Gallagher ... all round the side of the pitch.

Annette Clean and pretty children playing on the swings ...

Col Where did they come from?

Annette They're mine.

Col I don't want swings on my football pitch.

Annette No. It'll be too muddy.

Col It won't.

Annette On the football pitch.

Col It won't. Underground heating and highly paid groundsmen ...

Annette A hill with flowers on for them to run down ...

Col The groundsmen?

Annette I'll catch them at the bottom and swing them round. And put them in the swimming pool.

Col They'll never get any work done on my football pitch.

Annette Ouch.

Col What?

Annette It's kicking me.

Col What?

Annette The baby?

Col Kicking you?

Annette Yes. Look.

Col I can't see anything.

Annette Feel it.

She puts his hand on her stomach. He is fascinated

Col Striker.

Annette What?

Col He's a striker. I can tell by his action. Does it hurt?

Annette Sort of does. Sort of doesn't. (*She lies back*) I'd like a
golden bed. With a handsome prince in it.

Col I would. No, I wouldn't.

Annette Rich. He'd take me away from all this. And he'd love me.
That's what I'd like best in the world.

Col What I'd like best in the world is . . .

Annette What?

Col To have my mum back growing footballs under her dress.
Like you.

Annette Oh.

Col She went to heaven.

Annette That's nice.

Col Yes. Caught a twenty-seven bus.

They laugh at the joke

Arthur enters

(*To Annette*) So you just get off the tip, do you hear? Bloody
women. Nothing but trouble.

Arthur Don't shout at her, Col, she's pregnant.

Col That's because she's a woman. I know what we think of them,
eh, Art?

Arthur They're just people.

Col They're people who want to sleep in golden beds with rich
princes.

Annette I'd want him to love me.

Col I'd love you. No, I wouldn't.

Annette You wouldn't be any good in a golden bed. Neither
would you.

Arthur Good in any bed, me.

Teresa enters

Teresa I never met a man yet who didn't think he was good in bed.

Col I don't.

Teresa You're probably not.

Col I'm not.

Annette You probably are.

Col I'm no good at anything. I'm not even nice.

Teresa You really are a prick.

Arthur Men could be men if women only appreciated them.

Teresa (*to Col*) You probably are.

Col What we doing now, Arthur?

Arthur You can help me load this wardrobe, then I'm off. I'm off, Col, 'cos we've split. Remember?

Col I'm not helping you load it then.

Teresa I'll help you. Tit for tat, that's all.

They try and lift it

Jesus!

Annette Durrell's still in it.

Arthur opens the door. Long pause

Arthur He's dead.

Annette Oh, no! Durrell! (*She climbs in the wardrobe*)

Teresa Annette, love, be careful. You're treading on him.

Annette collapses on him, crying

Annette Durrell, don't be dead. You haven't been to the council yet. What am I going to do without you. You haven't looked after me. You haven't done anything yet.

Arthur Give him the kiss of life.

Col Who me?

Arthur I'll push on his chest. Go on.

Teresa helps Annette out of the wardrobe and the men try to revive Durrell

Annette He's so unreliable.

Teresa Men are. You have to learn to live without them.

Annette You can't have babies without them.

Teresa He's done that for you, love . . .

Col He'll miss the match on Saturday.

Annette He's probably not dead at all. He wasn't last time, was he? Durrell! (*She climbs back in the wardrobe*) Durrell, I do appreciate you. Where's his flask?

Col Here.

Annette tries to give Durrell a drink

He looks like a Villa shirt.

Annette He doesn't.

Col The colour of his face.

Annette Shut up.

Col A Villa shirt in a wardrobe.

Annette You're mad. Durrell's not going drinking with you again.

Col He can if he wants.

Annette No, he can't.

Arthur (*looking at Durrell*) No, he can't.

Teresa No, he can't.

Col No, he can't.

A long pause

Annette My baby won't have a dad. (*She sits on top of Durrell and strokes her stomach*) And no aunties and no uncles and no cousins.

Teresa Haven't you got any family?

Annette No grandmas and no grandpas. Durrell's got hundreds of family in Ireland, but I don't know where they are. I don't want to go to Ireland. I'm not Irish and I don't want an Irish baby.

Col I don't want to go to Ireland either.

Annette I don't know what to do.

Teresa Come home with me.

Annette Can I?

Teresa Of course you can. I'll be the baby's adopted grandma, if you like.

Annette That would be wonderful.

Arthur I'll be a grandpa, if you like.

Annette A grandma and a grandpa ... thank you.

Col (*very quietly*) I could be a dad if you like ...

Annette A grandma and a grandpa—oh thank you!

Arthur You can sit of a winter's evening and make rag mats.

Teresa And what will you be doing?

Arthur Waiting for you to come to bed ...

Annette If it's a boy, I'll call him Durrell. I'll call him Durrell, Durrell.

A long pause as Annette looks at the wardrobe

Col I could be a dad, if you like.

Annette Will you go to the council?

Col I'll tell them it's damp and the cooker doesn't work.

Annette And there's mould on the baby's things.

Col I'll tell them how little he is and that we've got to look after him.

Annette You'll take him to the football, won't you?

Col And the referee allows the game to go on, playing the advantage, and he dribbles the ball down the field, round the back of the last defender, passing to the inside, and the ball comes back and he heads it . . .

Arthur (*quietly*) Here we go, here we go, here we go . . .

Col Goal!

Teresa Come on, Annette, we'll take you home.

Arthur If we unload the van, we can put him in it.

Annette Leave him in the wardrobe—he likes it there.

Col Right.

They move off with Annette, chanting softly "Here we go", etc. The noise of the machines starts and the Lights begin to dim. There is a banging from the wardrobe and Durrell shouts. A crescendo of noise

Black-out

FURNITURE AND PROPERTY LIST

On stage: 3 plastic sacks
2 boots
Push-chair
Cooker
Football
Wardrobe (light-coloured/walnut)
Rubbish on tip

                  } old and battered

Off stage: Neck harness with bags hanging from it **(Teresa)**
Piece of broken china **(Col)**

Personal: **All characters:** sacks/bags
Durrell: 2 bottles of Guinness in pockets, cigarettes, hip flask

LIGHTING PLOT

To open: Lighting to silhouette figures on stage

Cue 1	**Col:** "Sit down then." *Reduce lighting*	(Page 8)
Cue 2	Noise increases *Black-out*	(Page 9)
Cue 3	The noise stops *Bring up lighting*	(Page 9)
Cue 4	Machine noise *Fade lights slowly to Black-out*	(Page 13)
Cue 5	When ready *Lights up*	(Page 13)
Cue 6	Machine noise *Fade lights to Black-out*	(Page 22)

EFFECTS PLOT

Cue 1   **Col:** "Sit down then."   (Page 8)
         Machine noise, increasing in volume

Cue 2   Black-out   (Page 9)
         Noise stops

Cue 3   **Durrell:** "Goal!"   (Page 13)
         Machine noise, increasing in volume

Cue 4   When ready   (Page 13)
         Noise stops

Cue 5   Characters move off chanting "Here We Go"   (Page 22)
         Machine noise, increasing in volume

MADE AND PRINTED IN GREAT BRITAIN BY
LATIMER TREND & COMPANY LTD PLYMOUTH

MADE IN ENGLAND